LOOK

AT THIS

F*CKING

HIPSTER

KING HIPSTER

Joe Mande

St. Martin's Griffin ☙ New York

For my family, who are proud of me

even though they really shouldn't be

Book design by Rich Arnold

www.stmartins.com

ISBN 978-0-312-62497-2

First Edition: April 2010

10 9 8 7 6 5 4 3 2

Introduction

Welcome to *Look at This F*cking Hipster,* your personal guide to understanding hipsters and hipster culture! In this book, we will explore hipsterdom in all its glorious facets and idiosyncrasies. And by "explore," I mean, of course, "ridicule." This book is chock-full of hipster ridicule. Why so much ridicule? Because . . . look at them. They're asking for it. It's like I always say: "Hipsters are ridiculous people, and you can't spell ridiculous without ridicule." . . . Or something.

Ugh, what am even I talking about?

Okay, look, I'll be honest. Even I can't believe my stupid-ass tumblr blog became a book. In fact, when I first met with my publishers, I asked them, "Why are you giving me a book deal? Who would buy a book full of content that's already on the Internet?" The head publisher quickly replied, "What's the Internet?" and then handed me a suitcase full of hundred-dollar bills. So, I guess that's how book deals happen.

I never expected my blog to become so popular. It started out as a joke, a pet project to amuse my friends and family. To be perfectly honest, my initial idea was to help my dad start a blog called IsThataHipster.com. Because whenever my parents visit me in Williamsburg, Brooklyn, that's what he asks me whenever a person walks by.

"Is that a hipster?"

"Yes. That's a hipster."

"Okay . . . but is that a hipster?"

"Yes, Dad. Pretty much everyone in this neighborhood is a hipster."

"What about that Asian guy over there? Can hipsters be Asian?"

"I suppose so, but they're usually white and have Asian girlfriends."

Exhibit A

The response to LATFH.com was immediate and overwhelmingly positive. Within a matter of days, my little joke had spread to millions of people all over the world. Unknowingly, I had tapped into something much larger than I could have ever expected—something retarded—that people from all corners of the globe yearned to laugh at and laugh with. Mocking hipsters, from their lifestyle choices to their fashion decisions to their inevitable offspring (yikes), has now become my full-time job. Some would say it's my duty.

I am not without my critics, however. Some readers have accused me of being a "monster," a "coward," a "hate-monger," and a "shitbird who eats bags of dicks." Others have called my blog the beginning of a "vast hate movement" that "promotes negativity and conformism." One idiot even called me the "Carlos Mencia of hipsters," which would be a super-offensive thing to say if it made any sense. Obviously, this is America, and everyone is entitled to have shitty opinions and no sense of humor. (But let me say that if my goal was to "promote" conformity, why would so many of the people I make fun of dress and behave in exactly the same way? That's just flawed logic.) Despite this, I would like to address these false charges right now by taking the opportunity to say right now, unequivocally: *I do not hate hipsters.* Let me repeat: *I do not hate hipsters.*

Now, don't get me wrong, I certainly don't love hipsters. That would be weird, like loving Scientologists or syphilis or something. But I don't hate them, either. I think that's important. I simply find the hipster lifestyle to be wildly fascinating. And if that sounds like I'm being condescending, that's because, yes, I'm being condescending. Duh, of course I am. But doesn't condescension come from a much better place than hatred? (That place = deez nuts.) I just think it's fair, after years and years of everyone making fun of poor white trash, that someone had the courage to stand up and make fun of rich white trash.

Other critics have told me that hipster bashing is "so four years ago" (which, ironically, is the most hipster-y thing a person could ever say). They claim that there's no such thing as a hipster, that it's simply an idea, a "fabricated social construct meant to demean and subjugate individualism and civil disobedience." To these people I say: Congratulations, you went to college! You totally know the terms "civil disobedience" *and* "social construct." Foucault the world, son!

The thing is, everyone goes to college. Everyone. Sorry, you're not special at all. Go snort some more Ritalin and jerk off to your Murakami collection. If there's one thing I'm certain of, it's that hipsters *do* exist. I live in Williamsburg, which is basically the Mecca for hipsters; the Bedford stop on the L train station is their Kaaba. Hipsters dominate my neighborhood. I smell their Tom's of Maine deodorant when I'm in line to get coffee in the morning. I hear them discuss the work of Krzysztof Kieślowski while I wait for the bus. I see them play organized kickball in the park. Adults. Playing kickball. And it's not just in Brooklyn. I've been exposed to hipsters in Philadelphia, Boston, San Francisco, Montreal, Los Angeles, Minneapolis, Kansas City, Baltimore, Austin, Moscow, London, in college town after college town . . . pretty much anywhere that (white) people live.

There's a hipster pandemic. They're spreading. They're multiplying. They're taking over. You might as well savor this moment while you can. Look at these fucking hipsters and laugh. Before it's too late.

1.

What Is a Hipster?

If you're reading this book right now, there's a good chance you yourself are a hipster and don't even know it. (Either that, or you're just wasting time at Urban Outfitters, waiting for your girlfriend to buy overpriced drapes or whatever.) Some of the biggest fans of LATFH.com also happen to be some of the biggest hipsters in the world. I've always found this a bit confusing. Do they like my Web site because they think it's funny? Do they like it because it feeds into their own sense of narcissism? Or do they actually hate the Web site, but are pretending to like it ironically? Are they being ironic ironically? Is that even possible? No one knows. That's the problem.

People are often surprised/disappointed when they meet me to learn that I'm not a hipster. They assume, because of my vast knowledge of the hipster world, that I must be deeply entrenched in that world, that I'm some trust fund baby with asymmetrical hair, trying to open my own art gallery and/or vegan unicorn cupcake shoppe. I suppose, in a way, that's sort of a compliment; only it's not at all.

I am not a hipster, and I say that with certainty. Just take a look at what's on my iPod; all you'll see is stuff like Earth, Wind & Fire, Prince, Chaka Khan, Luther Vandross—if anything, I'm a menopausal black woman.

I know I'm not a hipster, because being a hipster is a choice. Sure, I'll admit it: Like many people my age, I may have experimented a little bit in college. I vaguely remember nights sitting outside on a couch, drinking too much PBR and listening to the Libertines. But that's all ancient history now. I've seen the light since then. I've made the choice not to be a hipster. (Not that there's anything wrong with that! Honestly! Some of my best friends are hipsters!)

But what is a hipster, exactly? Well, the word "hipster" originated in the 1940s as a term to describe jazz enthusiasts who enjoyed smoking opium. (The same definition could apply to modern hipsters, only you'd have to replace "jazz" with "dance party" and "opium" with "salvia.") The term started to be used again about a half century later to describe a new batch of young people trying desperately to appear outside the mainstream.

Modern-day hipsters are unlike other youth-oriented countercultures of past generations—such as hippies, goths, and beatniks—because they don't really believe in anything. Hipsters have no overarching philosophy; there's no movement to the movement. In fact, a vast majority of hipsters refuse to admit that they're hipsters.[*] Most consider the term an insult, the equivalent of a racial slur.

---

[*] Seriously, though, I'm not a hipster. I have never once gone to see a band named after a deer or a wolf.

The only current event a hipster is concerned about is the "best new music" section on Pitchfork.com. The only human rights issue they can agree on is the inalienable right to act like a teenager well into your thirties.

Being a hipster is all about apathy. To belong, all you need is to show how little you care. But showing how little you care takes a lot of work, you guys! There are Girl Talk concerts you must attend, vintage clothes you have to buy, gallons of cheap whiskey and tasteless beer to be ingested. But, if you do it right, you'll be putting on airs of universal dispassion and nonchalance like a pro.

Exhibit B:
"What has two thumbs and access to his mom's credit cards?"

Everything they do is ironic; from the clothes they wear, to the TV shows they watch, to the stupid facial hair they grow—it's all an endless joke. There's no substance behind any of it. Hipsters rebel against a shallow, materialistic, directionless society by being shallow, materialistic, and directionless. It makes no sense. It's fighting conformity with conformity, not fitting in by fitting in. It just so happens that their specific type of conformity involves looking very silly. It's a community of unfocused people trying to out-silly each other. At the same time, however, they want to be taken seriously. Like I mentioned, hipsters all went to college and took Advanced Placement courses in high school, so they have strong opinions about books, art, politics, etc. They're philosophers and intellectuals who camouflage themselves as complete buffoons. As my comedian friend Hannibal Buress says, "It's cool if you have a handlebar mustache, but don't try to talk to me like you don't have a handlebar mustache."

Basically, hipsters are clowns—terrible, postmodern clowns who don't know any magic (except the old "disappearing eight ball" trick) and who get all upset and insolent when you point at them and laugh.

2.

What Makes a Hipster a Hipster?

The choice to become a hipster doesn't happen overnight. It's a gradual process, triggered often by loneliness, a fear of maturity, and/or emotional trauma. Becoming a hipster is kind of like joining a street gang, except there's no risk of violence and you have to pretend that you've read *Infinite Jest*. Typically, the metamorphosis into a hipster starts off slowly and with clear warning signs. However, if left unchecked, the sickness will begin to fester and metastasize rapidly. Soon, the victim will be almost impossible to recognize from his former self.

I know this for a scientific fact because I watched a friend become a hipster in front of my very eyes. One of my best friends from college, Josh, moved to New York shortly after experiencing a painful breakup (i.e., emotional trauma). Obviously, I was thrilled to have such a good friend suddenly living so close by. I couldn't wait to hang out with him, show him the city, get his mind off things. But as soon as Josh arrived in Brooklyn and settled in, I started noticing changes in his behavior.

He suddenly—and for no good reason—became a vegan, a far cry from the Atkins-diet meat-eating maniac I knew in college. At the time, I rationalized the decision, thinking maybe he'd found a new appreciation for healthy eating. I didn't say anything. Within a matter of weeks, Josh stopped wearing contacts, instead preferring to wear comically large wooden-frame eyeglasses. He grew a blond Larry Bird mustache. His jeans seemed to get tighter and tighter. A couple of months passed. Josh started smoking marijuana for the first time in his life, which was great, except he kept trying to get everyone to go on high adventures with him. He bought a rusty bicycle at a flea market and rode it around town wearing clothes he made himself. He recorded a two-disc concept album alone in his room using only toy instruments.

Again, despite my concerns, I said nothing. He was still mending a broken heart, I thought. He'll shape up anytime now. He must see how ridiculous he's being. A few weeks later, Josh got fired from his dog-walking job for being stoned, which he saw as a blessing, as it gave him more time to work on his art. His art, of course, being the crude, primitive tempera paintings of small forest animals that he applied directly onto the walls of his sublet apartment. To make money, Josh decided he would sell greeting cards on the street; these cards he made himself by tearing out photographs from old encyclopedias, gluing them onto note cards, then typing original poetry on the back using a typewriter he purchased at another flea market. He spent hours making his own peanut butter (when he wasn't in the midst of one of his frequent spicy lemonade master cleanses). By this point, Josh had been living in New York for almost a year. Things had gotten out of control. But just before I was able to sit Josh down and stage an intervention, he borrowed money from his parents and moved to Japan, where he now lives and plays in a diaper ukulele band. (That's a band wherein he and a bunch of Japanese dudes wear diapers and play ukuleles.)

This is an extreme example, but it's true and could just as well happen to someone you love, too. The following chapters will explore typical hipster lifestyle choices (aka "warning signs" or "symptoms"). If you suffer from one, or maybe two, of these examples, that doesn't automatically make you a hipster, but it definitely means you're flirting with disaster. Any more than that, you might as well pack up your ukulele and move to Japan.

"Why does everyone think we're models for Pantene Pro-HPV?"

Obnoxiously Large Glasses

"Yeah, they're pretty dope. I call them 'shades.'

You know, like, 'shades.' Get it? Oh, you do?

Well, my dad didn't. He hates me."

"She loves me not, she loves me not, she loves me not, she loves me not…"

"Do you guys like Wolf Parade?"

Obnoxiously Large Glasses

"The piercings were my orthodontist's idea."

"My face is all about

business in the front,

and party in the front."

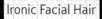
Ironic Facial Hair

"Okay. Here's one: Once upon a time, I stopped getting allowance."

FREE FAIRY TAILS

Tight Pants

"Trust me, girls love Chipmunks T-shirts. Very young girls."

Tight Pants

"It's safer if the natives give you toejobs."

Tight Pants

"Excuse me, sir. Could you spare some change? Please? I really need some help. My peacoat isn't red and it's ruining my whole aesthetic."

"My high school mascot was the Wolf Nipples, so …"

"Okay, check this out: it's the Virgin Mary in Ziggy Stardust makeup. Get it? You don't? Shit. I was hoping you could tell me why I did this to myself. Thanks, anyway."

"So, this is Bernini's famous statue 'Rape of Persephone' on my chest. I also have 'The Thinker' tattooed on my taint."

"No, I can't unbutton my top button. I'm shy."

Regrettable Tattoos

"It's weird that my 'Stay Clean' inner lip tattoo is always getting infected."

Dumb Haircuts

"I just want black teenagers to laugh at me on the subway. So, could you give me something similar to yours?"

Dumb Haircuts

"I'll only answer to the name Mrs. T."

Dumb Haircuts

"I might look like Kevin Federline, but I *eat* like Kevin Federline."

Dumb Haircuts

"My dream is to one day be in an abusive relationship with Wolverine."

Unexplainable Brand Loyalty To Pabst Blue Ribbon Beer

"I should totally Tweet about how cliché I'm being right now."

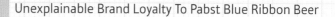
Unexplainable Brand Loyalty To Pabst Blue Ribbon Beer

"Now, this is what I call skull fucking."

"The back of my shirt says 'AND BEER AND WEED AND COKE AND SHROOMS AND PCP.'"

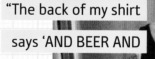

Yasser Arafat Scarves

"Yeah, I know this seat is reserved for disabled people. Look at me. This should count."

Yasser Arafat Scarves

"Hello, operator? Could you please tell me what the Cubs are?"

"Ugh, moving is the worst."

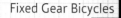
Fixed Gear Bicycles

"Shit. This is so embarrassing.
Before you take that picture,
hold on, let me make it look like
a V-neck. You got that? Good.
Phew! That was close."

Fixed Gear Bicycles

"I can never get the whole bike in my butt hole."

Thrift Store Clothes

"Dude, your dad is a doctor, right? Okay, because I found a bunch of bed bugs in my coat this morning. Could you ask him if they're technically coat bugs?"

"Nothing's better than relaxing after a long day of hunting on iPhone Oregon Trail."

Thrift Store Clothes

"I try to never discriminate.

That's why I have a ponytail

and a rat tail."

Thrift Store Clothes

"I seriously hope no one finds me here."

Thrift Store Clothes

"I'm just rehearsing my one-man musical, *Jesus Christ, I'm Such a Cunt Superstar*."

"If I had known I was coming to an art exhibition, I would have worn my Walgreens bag."

Homemade Clothes

"It's because my crotch, feet, torso, and shins are always cold, and my ankles, thighs, stomach, and forearms are always hot."

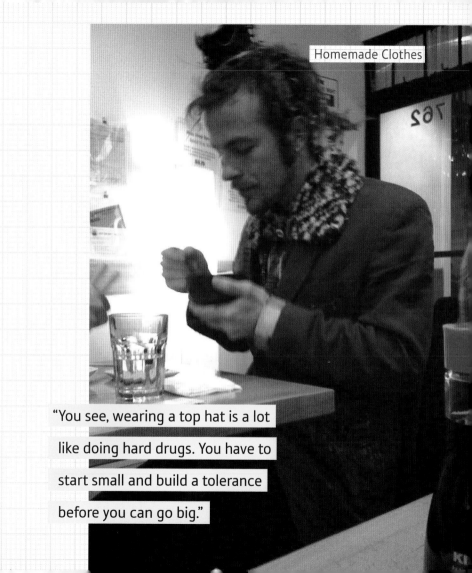

Homemade Clothes

"You see, wearing a top hat is a lot like doing hard drugs. You have to start small and build a tolerance before you can go big."

KISS MY HEIR-ASS

"What's your favorite part of the shirt I made? The pun that makes no sense, or the bedazzled stomach vagina?"

Homemade Clothes

"When life gives you ~~lemons~~ your dead grandma's drapes, make ~~lemonade~~ a tank top."

"It feels so liberating to finally leave home for the first time. No one telling me I can't ribbon-dance in flip flops. I'm a man now. I can ribbon-dance however I damn well please."

Generally Behaving Like A Child

"It's a total Tofurky sausagefest up in here."

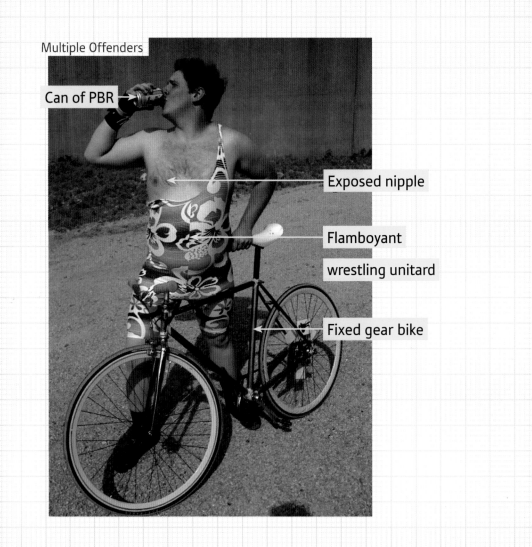

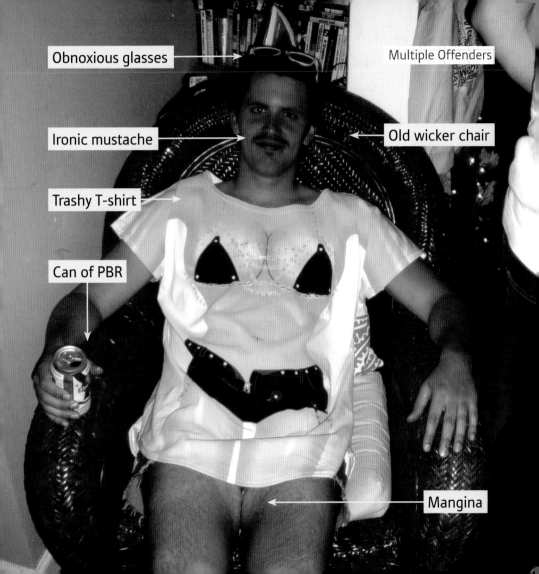

Obnoxious glasses

Multiple Offenders

Ironic mustache

Old wicker chair

Trashy T-shirt

Can of PBR

Mangina

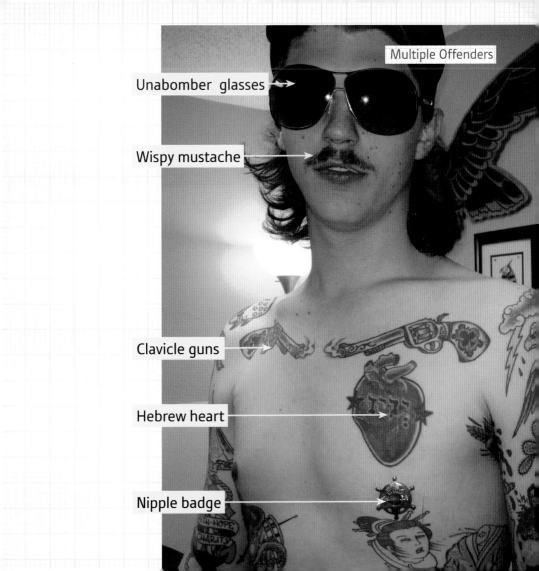

Unabomber glasses

Wispy mustache

Clavicle guns

Hebrew heart

Nipple badge

3.

Types of Hipsters

The way I see it, hipsters are a lot like cilantro. Personally, I don't enjoy the flavor of cilantro. I think it makes food taste like dish soap and the thought of eating dish soap is disgusting to me. Obviously, I'm not planning some massive crusade against cilantro, I'm just saying cilantro is not welcome in my kitchen (because my kitchen already has dish soap).

Now, I know some people love cilantro and that's fine. Why anyone would choose to eat something so undeniably unpleasant is a mystery to me, but I don't have a problem with it. We live in America, a country where people are allowed to ruin their food however they want.

Even so, my biggest problem with cilantro is that it keeps becoming more and more popular. It's a very trendy herb. The number of idiots who convince themselves that this dirty, tinny form of parsley is actually delicious and sophisticated grows exponentially every year. It's now gotten to the point that I can't buy a fucking burrito anymore without it being totally polluted with handfuls of these awful, metallic Palmolive flakes. And it's not just my precious burritos; cilantro has started creeping into the chili, the pad thai, even the pesto I eat at restaurants. I just wish we could go back to a simpler time, when cilantro was a shitty novelty for dum-dums and not the ghastly norm that everyone suddenly has to deal with.

The same goes with hipsters. Get these hipster burritos out of my face!

What's my point? Well, sometimes people think my definition of a hipster is too vague. For example, let's say I post a picture of this person:

I guarantee you that, within a few hours, I'll get fifteen nitpicky e-mails telling me, "Hey, that guy isn't a hipster, he's a *scenester*!" First of all, that's a guy? Second, fine, whatever, he's a scenester. Are you happy now? Of course you're not, because that's just giving a different name to the same thing. It's the same people who take off their plain white daytime V-necks and put on their glittery black nighttime V-necks. Hipsters are scenesters, scenesters are hipsters, and cilantro is coriander. Case closed.

But I don't mean to generalize. The truth is, there's a lot of diversity within the hipster/scenester/monster community. It's important to know all these subsets. Here are all the various types of hipsters.

"I've been the Yoko Ono to literally dozens of Brooklyn DJ collectives."

Asian Hispters

"OH MY GOD! DON'T TAKE MY PICTURE! Is your flash on? SERIOUSLY, DON'T! I'M A SHY PERSON! What's the aperture? Can you see my rings? STOP IT! I LOOK TERRIBLE!…"

"Look, I know what I'm doing. I'm a cute little 'China Girl' wearing David Bowie makeup. Do you know how many rich, femmy Jewish guys are going to buy me drinks tonight?"

Black Hipsters

"Now I'm co-opting *your* culture. How does it feel?"

"This is my Quincy Grace

Jones pose."

Hispanic Hipsters

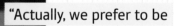

"Actually, we prefer to be called 'Hipspanics.'"

Hispanic Hipsters

"I can't believe I wore a bow tie. I feel so dressy."

Androgynous Hipsters

"I just hope my legs don't get a five o'clock shadow, too."

Androgynous Hipsters

"I'm sorry. This is the last time I'll ask, but…are we a lesbian couple? Even I can't tell."

"We're both big into MGMT and AARP."

Elderly Hipsters

"Do you like my CSS shirt? I love CSS. I have some CSS in my car. Would you like to see my CSS car? You'll have fun. It's full of CSS."

"This next song is called 'My Girlfriend Collects Dolls, But Is Still Way More Emotionally Mature Than I Am.'"

Musical Hipsters

"What am I doing out here?
I should just go home and
play Sitar Hero."

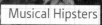

"When I play the recorder,

it's a space flute."

Musical Hipsters

"Please excuse my little purple blanket. It's just . . . whenever I play my little tiny guitar, I get a little tiny boner. It's a little embarrassing."

Dancing Hipsters

"Houston, we have a party."

Dancing Hipsters

"Wait, you wanted the girl to take her shirt off? Gross."

Dancing Hipsters

"I'm always ready for any situation, be it waiting tables, playing poker, running a 5K, or getting my pupils dilated."

Lesbian Hipsters

"I know this T-shirt seems a little crude, but it's actually an inside joke between the two of us. You see, 'cunt' is just my funny nickname for her…cunt."

Animal-Loving Hipsters

"I'm not going to let my pet pig stop me from buying used vinyl."

Animal-Loving Hipsters

"In honor of Bob Barker, we both got neutered."

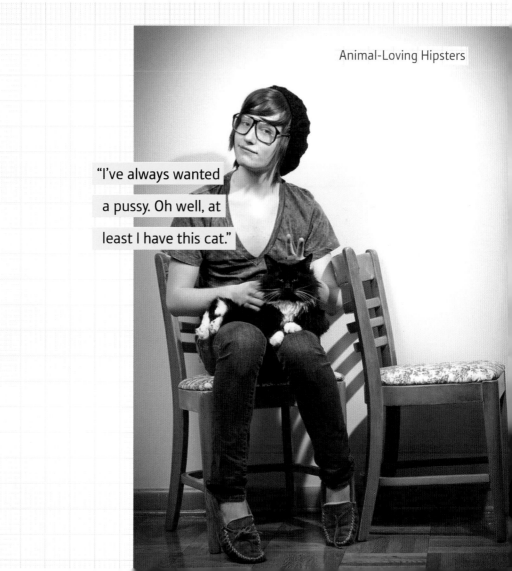

Animal-Loving Hipsters

"No, actually, he's caught
more diseases from me."

Suburban Wannabe Hipsters

"Do we have enough tickets to get that Brokencyde album?"

Let's Dress Up Like Indians Hipsters

"Here, have some cupcakes. Now give them back."

Let's Dress Up Like Indians Hipsters

"I'm going to smoke this dude's peace pipe tonight…if you know what I mean."

"I'm going to make it look

like you have smallpox!"

Let's Dress Up Like Indians Hipsters

"In our culture, we use every part of the Buffalo Exchange."

Let's Dress Up Like Indians Hipsters

"Do you know where I can trade wampum for whippits?"

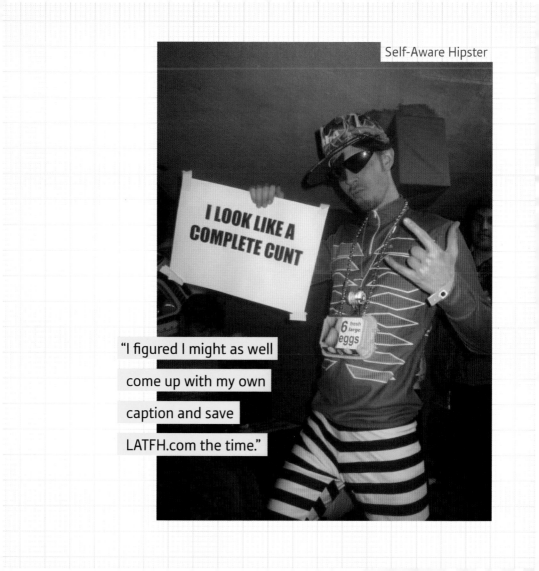

"I can't wait till we post this picture on Facebook. The Israeli government is going to shit its pants!"

Misguided Political Hipsters

"I like this outfit because it's so campy! Tranny concentration campy."

"How is it racist to be a fan of stars *or* bars? Those are like my two favorite things."

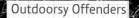

"I'm trying to do a Henry David Thoreau/Walden Pond type thing, only with GarageBand."

Outdoorsy Hipsters

"Seriously, if we went to Afghanistan, we'd laser tag the shit out of the Taliban."

Indoorsy Hipsters

"Note to self: Google 'Vampire-pattern baldness.'"

4.

Is This a Hipster?

Pop quiz, hotshot! Now that we've come this far, I think you're ready to take this thing to the next level. It's time to play my favorite game, "Is This a Hipster?"

The game is simple. You will be shown a series of pictures of human beings. Using your newfound knowledge of what makes a hipster a hipster and all the different types of hipsters, you must now try to correctly identify which of these humans are indeed hipsters. (Answers are located at the bottom of each page.)

Good luck! Readers who identify all twenty pictures correctly will win $1,000.*

---

*Correction: No one will be winning $1,000.

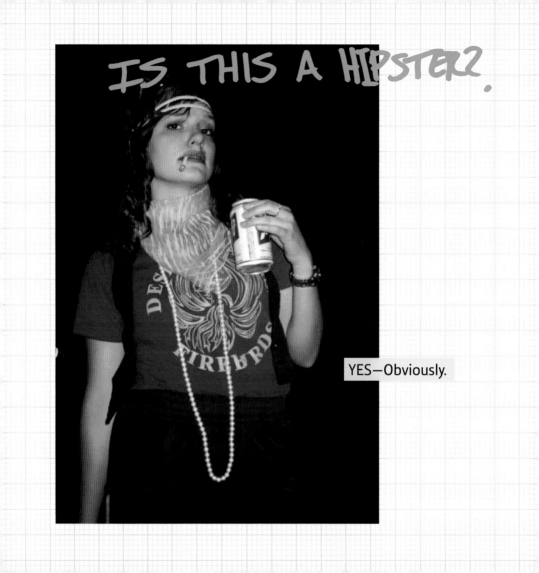

IS THIS A HIPSTER?

YES—Obviously.

IS THIS A HIPSTER?

YES—American Apparel

hoodie + no pants? Duh.

IS THIS A HIPSTER?

HADOUKEN!

NO—A hipster would not make his own Street Fighter 2 T-shirt, he would make his own Altered Beast T-shirt.

IS THIS A HIPSTER?

NO—That's a nightmare clown.

IS THIS A HIPSTER?

YES—Whether it's a man or woman, yes.

IS THIS A HIPSTER?

YES on the left. NO on the right.
(This is the kind of friendship and
understanding MLK, Jr., preached
about. [No it's not.])

IS THIS A HIPSTER?.

NO—That's a homeless superhero.

IS THIS A HIPSTER?

NO—That's a guy who should never be allowed anywhere near Disneyland.

IS THIS A HIPSTER?.

YES—He and Dr. Batting Helmet are a great couple.

IS THIS A HIPSTER?

YES—Who needs toilet paper when you can chill next to a pink bidet?

IS THIS A HIPSTER?

NO—That's a confused young woman who thinks she's an eight-year-old Japanese girl.

IS THIS A HIPSTER?.

YES—And I think he's my hero.

IS THIS A HIPSTER?

YES—That's DJ Hervé Villechaize.

IS THE **IPSTER?**

HARD TO TELL—It's probably a hipster, but it could be a woman with special needs who doesn't know how to put on a cardigan.

IS THIS A HIPSTER?

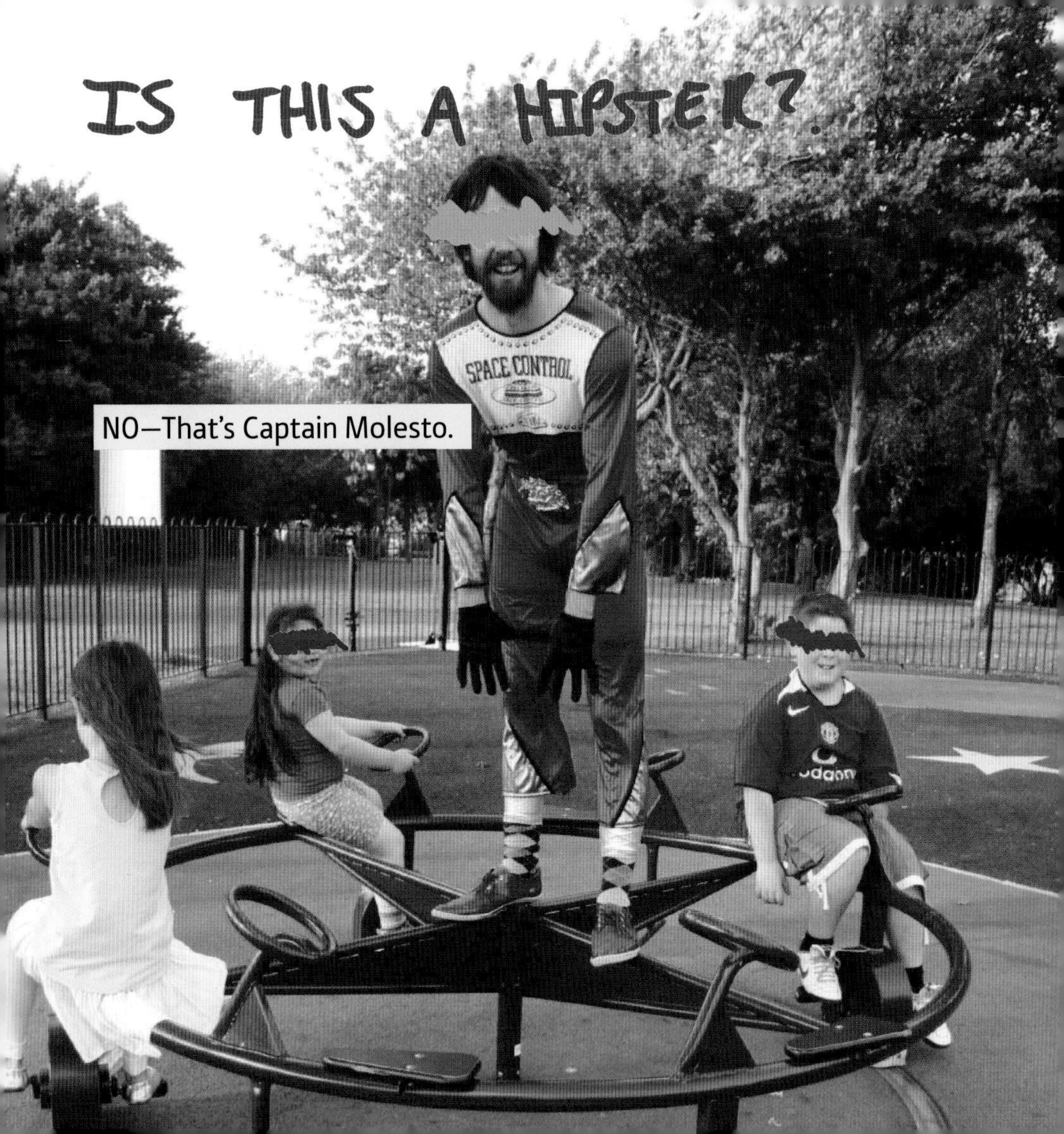

NO—That's Captain Molesto.

IS THIS A HIPSTER?!

NO—That's an IT nerd goofing around on his webcam between episodes of *Mythbusters*.

IS THIS A HIPSTER?.

YES—The saddest part is, she sleeps with her dealer for free catnip.

IS THIS A HIPSTER?

YES—This guy will write you a poem for $5, or for free, if you promise not to punch him in the face.

POEMS

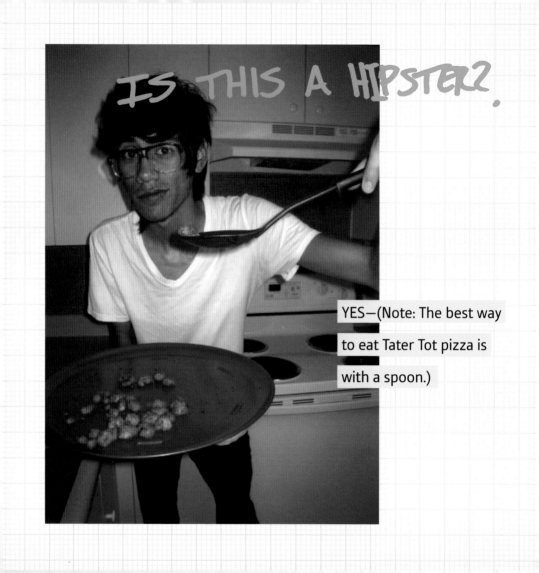

IS THIS A HIPSTER?

HARD TO TELL—Either this is a hipster who bought a piece of High School Musical merchandise for sardonic effect, or he's not a hipster and somewhere there's a dead twelve-year-old girl.

IS THIS A HIPSTER?

NO—Close, but no. These are actually very well-groomed douchebags. Slight difference.

IS THIS A HIPSTER?

YES—Either that, or that's the world's worst gang member.

5.

They're Just Like Us!

Though I give hipsters a hard time, it's important to remember that they too put on their jumpsuits one leg at a time. They are really no different than you or me. Just because their rent is usually paid for and they sleep through most of the day, that doesn't mean that the complications and minutiae of everyday life eludes them. Not at all. Hipsters are people, too.

The following is a fun collection of candid photographs that capture the ordinary, day-to-day existence of hipsters in the real world. You'll be sure to see that hipsters *really are just like us*!

They buy groceries!

They wash dishes!

They play video games!

They eat brunch!

They celebrate Christmas!

They use ATMs!

They dance on ATMs!

They scrawl drunken messages with chalk on the floors of subways!

They skateboard behind baby strollers!

They dress up like spies and go to Pinkberry!

They play drums in the ocean!

They get married in front of bleak, desert-themed elementary school murals!

They think beer emits a Wi-Fi signal!

They get demon boners!

They relax in their face paint, rubber gloves, and skull hats!

They leisurely read a pretentious book

while they sit next to a sign they made

asking people to give them money so they

can take a girl out on a concert date!

6.

Celebrity Hipsters

Imagine being a celebrity in the twenty-first century. Sure, the fame and fortune sounds nice, but it comes at a price. It's a lifestyle fraught with difficulties and pressures. Your every move is tracked and documented by a pack of blood-hungry, ever-vigilant paparazzi whose objective is to discover your secrets, expose your frailties, and destroy everything you've worked so hard to achieve. You can't escape it. The despicable tabloid media, with its twenty-four-hour news cycle, is devoured on a minute-by-minute basis by the very same celebrity-obsessed society that put you in this position of recognition and acclaim in the first place. You can't trust these people. Sure, your fans might be fine for the most part, but there are those twisted few who love you so much that they want to hurt you. So you hire bodyguards; you build a fortress; you use your material wealth to insulate yourself from a cruel and bitter world . . . only to get lambasted by the press for being paranoid and out of touch. Then there's the entertainment business itself, with all its pitfalls and the snakes who go after your money, all of them lying to you, inflating your ego, warping your personality. You feel the pressure to stay beautiful, keep skinny, and look young forever.

Just imagine that weight on your shoulders—all the angst and suspicion you would feel. What would you do? Would you go crazy and start dressing up like a complete jackass? Because that's what these people did. Here's a list of Hollywood's biggest hipsters.

Vincent Gallo

"I'm currently writing *Brown Bunny 2*. This time, it'll be two hours of me getting a blowjob and then three minutes of me driving in a car."

Chloë Sevigny

"I can't wait to be in

Brown Bunny 2!"

Mary-Kate Olsen

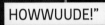
"Are you going to make

fun of my outfit?

HOWWUUDE!"

Zachary Quinto

"BEAM ME UP, VON DUTCH!"

Russell Brand

"America didn't have proper dick jokes before I came here, inn'itt? Ha! Did you catch that? Before I came here. Because of ejaculation, inn'itt?"

Drew Barrymore

"I went to face-paint school (rehab) when I was eleven."

Adrien Brody

"Whatever, bro. I'm still getting laid from that Holocaust movie!"

Tilda Swinton

"I'll give you one hint to what's under this kilt: it's my albino penis."

Joaquin Phoenix

7.

Hipsters Through the Ages

Through my extensive research for this book (i.e., getting stoned while reading Wikipedia) I discovered that the hipster aesthetic is really an amalgamation of styles that could be traced back decades, even centuries. Hipsters try, and fail, to capture the looks and personalities of times gone by. It's sort of sad, when you think about it.

There are certain historical figures who, if they used a time machine and found themselves at an Echo Park pool party tomorrow, would fit right in. These are those figures.

Jesus Christ (0–33)

Jewish carpenter, healer of the sick, son of God. *If he was around today*: He'd be in the Peace Corps and turning water into Sparks.

Rasputin (1869–1916)

Syphilitic Russian mystic, friend and adviser to Czar Nicholas II. *If he was around today*: He'd be a member of the Fleet Foxes.

Joseph Stalin (1878–1953)

Former communist leader of the U.S.S.R. *If he was around today*: He would institute a Five-Year Plan to build the country's biggest farmer's market. (When the market inevitably fails to make a profit, the farmers will all be shot in the head and buried in a mass grave.)

James Joyce (1882–1941)
Famous Irish author and
poet. *If he was around today*:
He'd be writing scripts with
Diablo Cody.

Salvador Dali (1904–1989)
Revolutionary surrealist
painter. *If he was around
today*: He'd be in an open
relationship with this person.

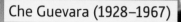

Che Guevara (1928–1967)

Author, statesman, Marxist

revolutionary. *If he was around*

today: He'd be involved in Ralph

Nader's 2012 campaign.

Buddy Holly (1936–1959)
Rock and Roll pioneer. *If he was around today*: He'd be working part-time at an art house theater and playing for change in the Prospect Park subway station.

Janis Joplin (1943–1970)

A blues/folk singer who sang with an over-the-top affected voice, drove around in a Porsche art-car, and died from alcohol and drug abuse. *If she was around today*: Same.

Rollie Fingers: (1946–Present) Hall of Fame relief pitcher. *If he was around today*: He'd be the captain of his kickball team and a freelance party photographer for his Web site, LastNightsFingerblast.com.

Everyone on *Scooby-Doo* (1969–Who cares?)
For-hire teenage detective agency. *If they were
around today*: They would be using the Mystery
Machine to sell weed around town and to
occasionally help friends move.

8.

Look at These Fucking Love Connections

Mother Teresa once said, "If I love until it hurts, then there is no hurt, but only more love." Coming from a woman with her hymen intact, these are wise words indeed. It's true: Everyone deserves to be loved, even hipsters.

I don't want to brag, but I must admit I have a special knack for matchmaking. What can I say? It's a gift. I'm able to find people with unique, often strange compatibilities, and I bring them together. Granted, I do it using Photoshop, but it's the same principle.

Here are some of the people I've brought together. For the sake of mankind, let's just hope they use protection.

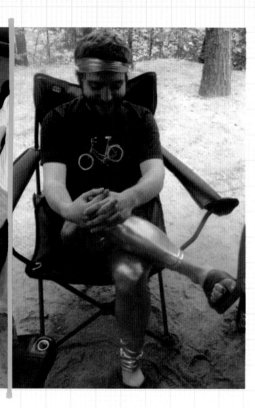

Look at this fucking color-coordinated connection.

Look at this fucking

eyewear connection.

Look at this fucking

Alaskan connection.

Look at this potential unicorn threesome.

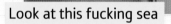

Look at this fucking sea captain connection.

Look at this fucking
keyboard connection.

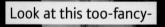

Look at this too-fancy-for-public-transportation connection.

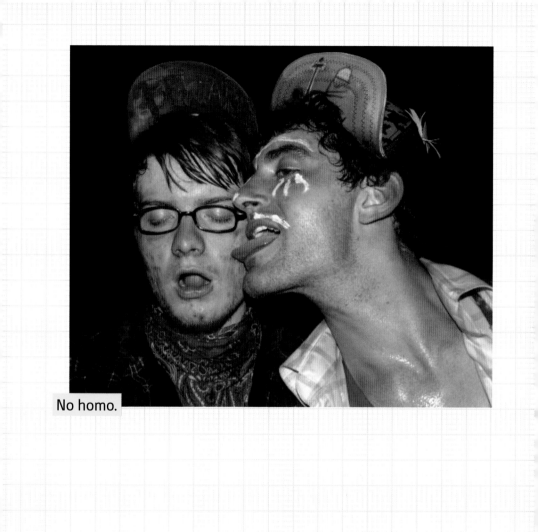

No homo.

No homo.

No Jews, no homo.

No homo.

No homo.

No homo.

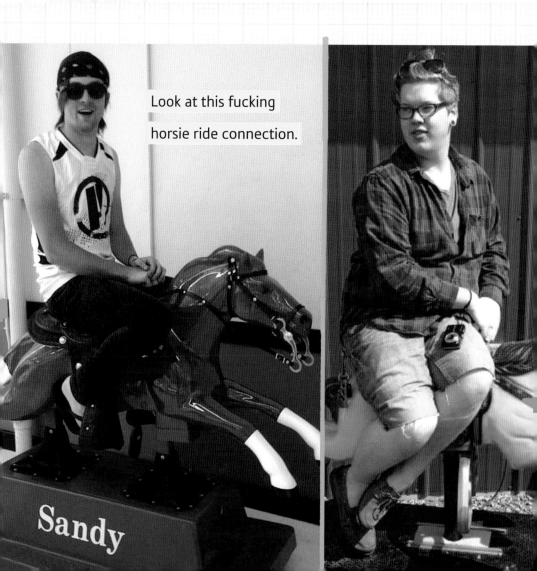

Look at this fucking horsie ride connection.

Sandy

Look at this potential biracial foursome.

Look at this fucking firearm connection.

Look at this fucking codpiece connection.

Look at this fucking crucifix connection.

Look at this fucking

creepy kabuki connection.

9.

Beeeeeaaaaaaans

Personally, my favorite thing about the LATFH experience (after the whole "getting paid" thing) has been the saga of a man named Beans.

It all started on April 29, 2009, when I posted this picture:

"Excuse me, ladies and gentlemen. I'm sorry to interrupt whatever kind of stupid street fair this is, but I need your attention for one moment. I've lost my little brother. I was over there buying a gyro and, while my back was turned, he simply disappeared. So, if everyone could please just keep an eye out for my brother. His name is Russell, but everyone calls him 'Beans' for short. He kind of looks like me, but with longer hair and a bigger beard. Oh, and he doesn't wear glasses. Actually, he doesn't wear much of anything. Basically, you should all be looking for a big fat dude wearing little boy's underwear and high-top sneakers. Beeeeeaaaaans! Beans, wheeeere aaaaare yoooou?"

I found myself mesmerized by this photograph. I stared at it for hours. However, the longer I stared, the more questions I had. Who was this magical Beans character? What was going on inside that big hairy head? Where are his clothes? Is he braiding his chest hair?

Needless to say, Beans was an instant Internet celebrity. Within hours, readers started sending me e-mails, recounting their own personal Beans experiences, attaching photographic evidence of Beans sightings for me to analyze.

Exhibit C:
A typical Beans sighting

Beans became something like a hipster Bigfoot, only hairier and way more photogenic. Fans of Beans wrote to me frequently, aggressively demanding more Beans. Paradoxically, the more pictures I posted of Beans, the farther away he seemed from me. I knew I needed to find Beans myself, become Beans's friend, and publish a book about him.

So that's exactly what I did. I found Beans on Facebook and invited him to take part in a tasteful professional photo shoot. Beans said yes, and showed up at the studio that Saturday with a bag full of costumes. I told Beans he could do whatever he wanted, and he did just that. The following are pictures from that extraordinary event.

I'm not even sure if Beans is a hipster. But it doesn't matter. He's so much more than that. He's majestic.

"BEEEEEEEEEANS

HUUUUUUUNNNGRRYYY!"

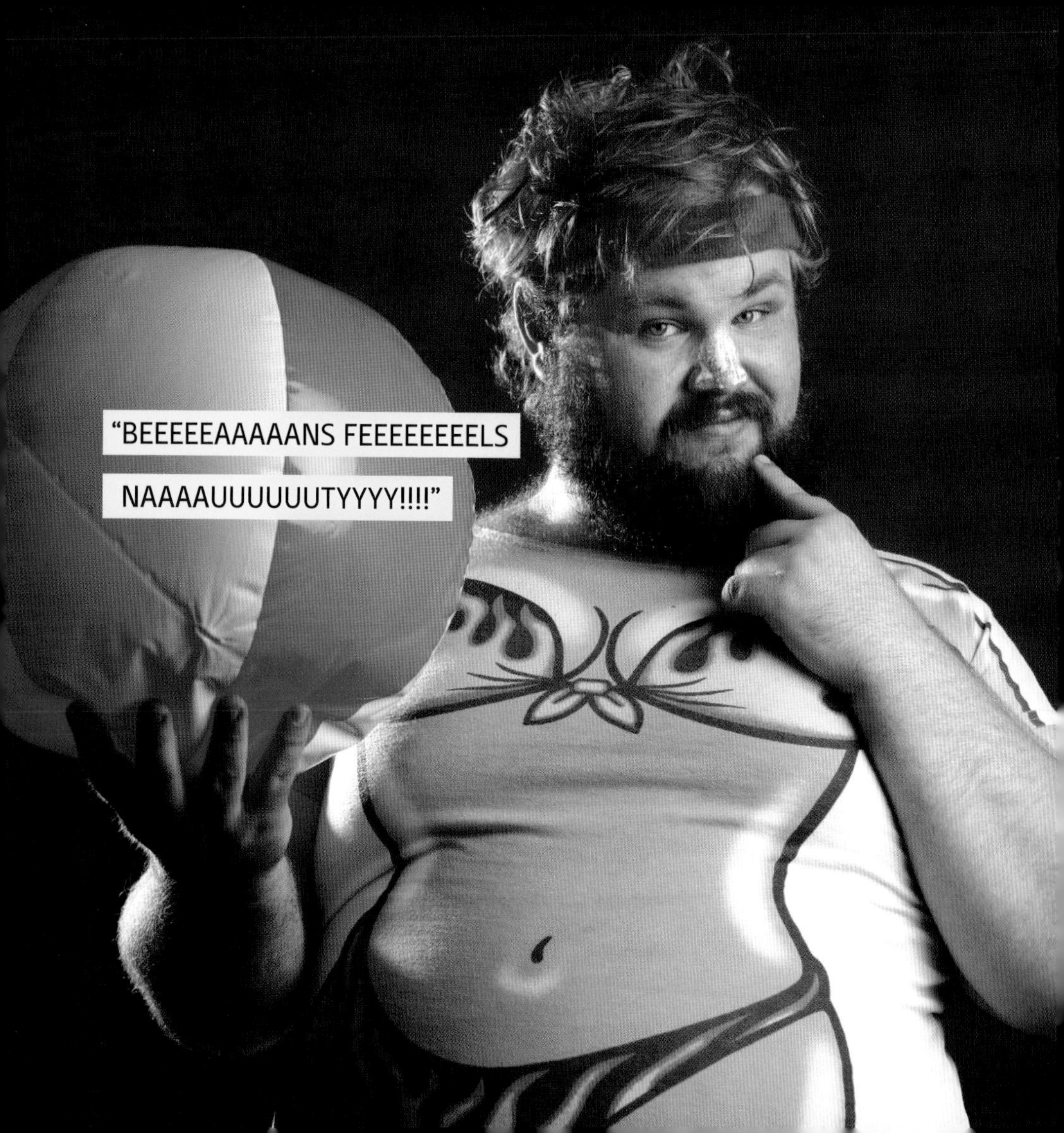
“BEEEEEAAAAANS FEEEEEEEELS
NAAAAUUUUUTYYYY!!!!”

"BEEEEEAAAAAAAAANS PLEEEEEEEDGE
AAAAALLEEEEEGIAAAANCE TOOOO THEEEEE
FLAAAAAAAAG OOOOOF THEEEEEE
UUUUUUUNIIIIIIIITED STAAAAAAATESSS OOOOOOF
AAAAAAAMMMEEEEERRRRIIIIICAAAAAAAA!!!"

"BEEEEEAAAAAAAAAANS

DEEEEEEEPRRREEEEEESSSSED!!!"

"BEEEEEEAAAAAAANS

DAAAAAAAAAMAAAAAGED

FOOOOOOOR LIIIIIIIIIFE!!!"

10.

Conclusion

Well, that's it. You've come to the end of the *Look at This F*cking Hipster* book. I trust you've enjoyed yourself and let out a few hearty laughs in the process. What's most important, though, is that you've come away knowing a great deal more about hipsters and hipsterdom. Just kidding! You have learned absolutely nothing from reading this book! (And, honestly, if you're upset about that, you should ask yourself why you were trying to learn anything from a picture book with the word "F*cking" in the title. Dumbass.)

You know, I hope that, if anything, this book helps to squelch all the hipster hatred out there in the world, not promote it. Hipsters really aren't that bad. And they're here to stay. It's now up to the rest of us to learn to accept it. What we're witnessing is a cultural shift. It's a natural evolutionary progression, or perhaps a new type of groupthink, that helps people avoid the pressures of real life by normalizing and extending mental juvenescence well beyond physical juvenescence. If 40 is the new 30, then I guess 30 is the new 15.

Is it annoying to overhear some pretentious jerk with a wispy mustache talk about his graphic novel adaptation of *The Fountainhead*? Of course it is. That guy is awful. But you must keep things in perspective. It's not like *Waterworld* has happened yet. We don't all live on floating piles of garbage in the ocean, worried that filthy pirates will barge in on their Jet Skis and rape us for our cigarettes and mason jars full of dirt. No. We'll leave all that for our grandchildren to deal with.

Luckily, we live in a world where becoming a hipster is a choice—deliberate or not—made by rational adults. But I worry for the future. I see a new dark age approaching, where that choice is taken away. A day when children are taught to mistrust mainstream music, unused clothing, or anything cooked with gluten. A grim wasteland where babies smoke tiny Parliaments and go to sleep with the $33\frac{1}{3}$ series as their only bedtime stories. A new generation without any values, groomed into a counterculture with no knowledge of the culture against which they counter.

When that terrible day arrives, I don't know what I'll do. Will I set myself on fire like the monk on the cover of that Rage Against the Machine album? Or will I just give myself up to the hipster babies, letting them rip the flesh from my body, like piranhas do to a goat, until all that's left of me is my gleaming white skeleton? (Sorry, I forgot to mention, they'll all be cannibals.)

Yes, that will be a sad, sad day indeed.

"Meat! Meat! Meat! Meat! Meat! Meat! Meat!"

Caption	Photo Credit
"White and have Asian girlfriends."	Anonymous
"What has two thumbs . . ."	Michael Schulz
"Why does everyone think . . . ?"	Anonymous
"Yeah, they're pretty dope. . . ."	Helena Wyche
"She loves me not . . ."	Anonymous
"Do you guys like Wolf Parade?"	Anastasia Zavgorodni
"The piercings were my orthodontist's idea."	Gregoire Muise
"My face is all about . . ."	Anonymous
"Okay. Here's one: Once upon a time . . ."	Thomas Fone
"Why yes, I *do* have ironic pubic hair as well."	Dennis Verrelli
"Trust me, girls love Chipmunks T-shirts . . ."	Anonymous
"It's safer if the natives give you toejobs . . ."	Douglas Keller
"Excuse me, sir. Could you . . ."	Yelena Grinberg
"My high school mascot . . ."	Anonymous
"Okay, check this out . . ."	Emma Freed
"So, this is Bernini's famous statue . . ."	Lauren Sanders
"No, I can't unbutton my top button . . ."	Lauren Sanders
"It's weird that my 'Stay Clean' . . ."	Kristyn Solie
"I just want black teenagers to laugh at me . . ."	Anonymous
"I'll only answer to the name Mrs. T."	Samantha Brustin
"I might look like Kevin Federline . . ."	Clint House
"My dream is to one day . . ."	Anonymous

Caption	Photo Credit
"I'M THE KING OF THE WORST!"	Tegan Snyder
"I should totally Tweet . . ."	Ricardo Melgarejo
"Now, this is what I call skull fucking."	Anonymous
"The back of my shirt says . . ."	Zac from the Boyertown Goof Squad
"Yeah, I know this seat is reserved . . ."	Joanne DeVault
"Why does everyone think we'd be naturally . . ."	Anonymous
"Hello, operator? Could you please . . ."	Alicia Eckert
"Ugh, moving is the worst."	Patrick Lawler
"Shit. This is so embarrassing . . ."	Noah Benjamin
"I can never get the whole bike . . ."	Kelsie Rotkel
"Dude, your dad is a doctor, right? . . ."	Anonymous
"Nothing's better than relaxing . . ."	Anonymous
"I try to never discriminate . . ."	Laura Sievers
"I seriously hope no one finds me here."	Chalotte Law
"I'm just rehearsing my one-man musical . . ."	Anonymous
"If I had known I was coming . . ."	Andrew D.
"It's because my crotch, feet, torso . . ."	Taylor P.
"You see, wearing a top hat . . ."	Lauren Rothman
"What's your favorite part of the shirt . . ."	Aesha Waks
"When life gives you . . ."	Anonymous
"It feels so liberating to finally leave home . . ."	Nathan Van Fleet
"It's a total Tofurky sausagefest up in here."	Gray Thorton
Flamboyant wrestling unitard.	Walter Hamilton

Caption	Photo Credit
old wicker chair	Mike Baker
drinking beer out of a straw like an alcoholic child	Hailey Thompson
Unabomber glasses	Kali Ann Kirchner
hipster/scenester	Vanessa Valdes
"I've been the Yoko Ono . . ."	Anonymous
"OH MY GOD! DON'T TAKE . . ."	Katzi Roman
"Look, I know what I'm doing . . ."	KittyLili
"Now I'm co-opting your culture . . ."	Alana de Haan
"This is my Quincy Grace Jones pose."	Anonymous
"How is it that I'm the dude . . ."	Anonymous
"Actually, we prefer to be called 'Hipspanics.'"	Dan Euto
"I can't believe I wore a bow tie. I feel so dressy."	Sergio Guadarrama
"I just hope my legs don't get . . ."	Anonymous
"I'm sorry. This is the last time I'll ask . . ."	Jennifer Scully
"We're both big into MGMT and AARP."	Patrick Lawler
"Do you like my CSS shirt? . . ."	Tayyib Smith
"This next song is called . . ."	Thomas Fone
"What am I doing out here? . . ."	aljuk
"When I play the recorder, it's a space flute."	Nicki Hechinger
"Please excuse my little purple blanket . . ."	Anonymous
"Houston, we have a party."	Mike C. and April M.
"Wait, you wanted the girl . . ."	Anonymous
"I'm always ready for any situation . . ."	Luke Stoller

Caption	Photo Credit
"I know this T-shirt seems a little crude …"	Jamie Joong
"I'm not going to let my pet pig …"	Debby Cho
"In honor of Bob Barker, we both got neutered."	Holly Bowden
"I've always wanted a pussy …"	Noelle White
"No, actually, he's caught more diseases from me."	Rebecca Tharp
"Do we have enough tickets …"	Anonymous
"Here, have some cupcakes …"	Jordan Musenbrock
"I'm going to smoke this dude's peace pipe …"	Nicole Klepper
"I'm going to make it look like you have smallpox!"	Mawiyah Lythcott
"In our culture, we use …"	Nick Anzaldua
"Do you know where I can trade …"	Anonymous
"I figured I might as well …"	Ed Lomas
"I can't wait till we post this picture …"	Anonymous
"I like this outfit because …"	Anonymous
"How is it racist to be a fan of stars *or* bars? …"	Anonymous
"I'm trying to do a Henry David Thoreau …"	Josh Koenig
"Seriously, if we went to Afghanistan …"	Jessica Boddorff
"Will you hold my purse? …"	Patricija Kirvaitis
"Note to self: Google …"	DPOG
YES—Obviously.	Liz Wilshin
YES—American Apparel hoodie …	Alison Buatti
NO—A hipster would not …	Jesse Proulx
NO—That's a nightmare clown.	Aleck Davis

Caption	Photo Credit
YES—Whether it's a man or woman.	Pax Rasmussen
YES on the left. NO on the right . . .	Patrick Marshall
NO—That's a homeless superhero.	Anonymous
NO—That's a guy . . .	Anonymous
YES—He and Dr. Batting Helmet . . .	Bob Ailstock
YES—Who needs toilet paper . . .	Luis Lopez
NO—That's a confused young woman . . .	Kaley Hall
YES—And I think he's my hero.	Anonymous
YES—That's DJ Hervé Villechaize.	Alison Buatti
HARD TO TELL—It's probably . . .	Anonymous
NO—That's Captain Molesto.	Loreana Rushe
NO—That's an IT nerd . . .	Gina Cacace
YES—The saddest part . . .	Anonymous
YES—This guy will write you a poem . . .	Sarah Karp Ward
YES—(Note: The best way . . .)	Steven Ospina
HARD TO TELL—Either this is a hipster . . .	Jennifer Neis
NO—Close, but no . . .	Alana de Haan
YES—Either that, or . . .	Anonymous
They buy groceries!	Anonymous
They wash dishes!	Andy Sauls
They play video games!	Jesus Diaz
They eat brunch!	Andre O. Hoilette
They celebrate Christmas!	Brandon Veski

Caption	Photo Credit
They use ATMs!	Andrew
They dance on ATMs!	Matthew Zdano
They scrawl drunken messages . . .	Bryan Wall
They skateboard behind baby strollers!	Eliina M. Viele
They dress up like spies and go to Pinkberry!	Rachel Elias
They play drums in the ocean!	JoeVele@discosalt.com
They get married in front of . . .	Keara Ross
They think beer emits a Wi-Fi signal!	I. Whitington
They get demon boners!	Matt Gzowski
They relax in their face paint . . .	Maria Suzanne Johnson
They leisurely read a pretentious book . . .	Greg Bigoni
"I'm currently writing *Brown Bunny 2* . . ."	John Sciulli/WireImage
"I can't wait to be in *Brown Bunny 2*!"	Bennett Raglin/WireImage
"Are you going to make fun . . ."	Dimitrios Kambouris/WireImage
"BEAM ME UP, VON DUTCH!"	Michael Tran/FilmMagic
"America didn't have proper dick jokes . . ."	Jean Baptiste Lacroix/WireImage
"I went to face-paint school . . ."	Tim Mosenfelder/Getty Images
"Whatever, bro. I'm still getting laid . . ."	Florian Seefried/Getty Images
"I'll give you one hint . . ."	ChinaFotoPress/Getty Images
"I'm a rapper."	Bruce Gifford/FilmMagic
Jesus Christ	Burstein Collection/Corbis
Rasputin	Popperfoto/Getty Images
Joseph Stalin	Akg-images/RIA Nowosti/The Image Works

Caption	Photo Credit
James Joyce	Topham/The Image Works
Salvador Dali	Hulton Archive/Getty Images
Che Guevara	Joseph Scherschel/Time Life Pictures/Getty Images
Buddy Holly	General Artists Corporation/Getty Images
Janis Joplin	Stroud/Express/Getty Images
Rollie Fingers	Focus on Sport/Getty Images
Everyone on *Scooby-Doo*	Hanna-Barbera/Everett Collection
Look at this fucking color-coordinated connection.	(1) Anonymous (2) Anonymous
Look at this fucking eyewear connection.	(1) Florence Foley (2) Jaik Miller
Look at this fucking Alaskan connection.	(1) Malik Samsess (2) Cesar Perez
Look at this potential unicorn threesome.	(1) Anonymous (2) Charlotte Law (3) Samantha Stern
Look at this fucking sea captain connection.	(1) Clint House (2) Anna Triporin
Look at this fucking keyboard connection.	(1) Anonymous (2) Anonymous
Look at this too-fancy . . .	(1) Roy Capulet (2) Esmeralda Rupp-Spangle
No homo 1	Anonymous
No homo 2	Cassie K.
No Jews, no homo.	Gabrielle Tousignant
No homo 3	Megan McCormick
No homo 4	Ross Cook-Golbsh
No homo 5	Katie Batten

Caption	Photo Credit
Look at this fucking horsie ride connection.	(1) Anonymous
	(2) Alexandra Spurlock
Look at this potential biracial foursome.	(1) Anonymous (2) Steve Lieb
Look at this fucking firearm connection.	(1) Alison Buatti (2) James Swann
Look at this fucking codpiece connection.	(1) Anonymous) (2) Charlotte Law
Look at this fucking crucifix connection.	(1) Anonymous (2) Kat Bee
Look at this fucking creepy kabuki connection.	(1) Jon Stefan (2) Anonymous
"Excuse me, ladies and gentlemen . . ."	Michael Horowitz
A typical Beans sighting.	Josh Chaplin
"BEEEEEEEEEEANS HUUUUUUUNNNGRRYYY!"	Seth Olenick
"BEEEEEAAAAANS FEEEEEEEELS . . ."	Seth Olenick
"BEEEEEAAAAAAAANS PLEEEEEEEDGE . . ."	Seth Olenick
"BEEEEEAAAAAAAAAANS DEEEEEEEPRRREEEEEEESSSSSED!!!"	Seth Olenick
"BEEEEEEAAAAAAANS DAAAAAAAAAMAAAAAGED . . ."	Seth Olenick
"Meat! . . ."	Sachi Devidasi Maclachlan

Acknowledgments

For my family, who are proud of me even though they really shouldn't be. Thanks to everyone who helped make this book a surreality: Anne and Kara at Generate, Hannah Gordon at Foundry, Yaniv at SMP, all the contributing photographers, the wonderful people at Tumblr, Noah Garfinkel and Hannibal Buress for their insights, Nick Kroll and John Mulaney for calling me an idiot, Kylie Augustine for telling me to calm down, Seth Olenick, Rory Walsh, Darren Mabee, the crazy guy who contacted publishers pretending to be me, my "followers" (gross), and to hipsters worldwide for being such easy targets.

Joe Mande lives in New York City, where he works as a writer and comedian. He was named "Best New Comedian" by *Time Out New York* and appears on Comedy Central and Vh1's "Best Week Ever." He has never once gone to see a band named after a deer or a wolf. For more, check out JoeMande.com.